CW01429919

ELEVATE

THE HEALING
Power OF Tea

Blends for health and wellness

Published by Hinkler Pty Ltd
45–55 Fairchild Street,
Heatherton Victoria Australia
www.hinkler.com

hinkler

© Hinkler Pty Ltd 2022

Author: Shauna Reid
Internal design: Lisa Robertson
Cover design and illustrations: Rachael Jorgensen

Images © Hinkler Pty Ltd or Shutterstock.com

ISBN: 978 1 4889 0483 7

Printed and bound in Malaysia

ELEVATE

THE HEALING
Power OF Tea

Blends for health and wellness

Shauna Reid

h

hinkler

CONTENTS

Introduction

A cup of tea is one of life's simple yet powerful pleasures. For thousands of years, people have brewed and drunk tea in thousands of different ways, enjoying it for healing, nourishment and connection. It's no wonder that tea is the second most widely consumed beverage in the world, after water.

Tea can help boost a bad day, soothe a sore tummy, lull you to sleep, or accompany a chat with a friend. Whether it's a strong mug of black tea to start the day, an invigorating infusion of fresh herbs, or a delicate Darjeeling at afternoon tea time, there's a tea out there to suit every moment.

Tea is…

… A health and wellbeing boost. From the antioxidant riches of true teas to the healing properties of botanical infusions, people have drunk tea for centuries to feel good and find relief from ailments of all kinds.

… An exciting world of flavour. From just one single plant called *Camellia sinensis* comes the contrasting deliciousness of black, white, green and oolong teas. Then herbal teas bring a whole lot more tastiness to the party with flowers, herbs and spices.

… A moment of rest and reflection. Tea is like an escape hatch in the middle of your day that you can retreat to anytime. You can drink tea at work, in the car, in the garden, in your bed, in a crowd or by yourself. It's always a good time for a tea break!

… A conduit to connection. Tea brings people together, from a fancy high tea to a quick work break cuppa or a heart-to-heart chat with a loved one. In our busy world, the simple act of making and drinking tea is an everyday moment of shared humanity.

… A simple shortcut to self care. All you need is some tea, hot water and a mug and you're on your way to a nurturing moment of real self care that's equally good for your mind and body.

In this book you'll learn all about tea and its wonderful healing powers for the mind, body and spirit. We'll explore:

- **Tea basics.** Learn about different categories of tea, from true teas to herbal tisanes and blends. Discover how tea became popular and how those humble green leaves are processed into the beverage we know and love.
- **How to make a great cup of tea.** Try the ten simple steps that elevate tea from good to amazing!
- **Tea for health and wellbeing.** From the powerful properties of true teas to the natural healing of botanical tisanes, discover how tea can give your health a boost.
- **Tea for self care.** Learn why tea is one of the most fun and doable ways to practise self care and mindfulness.
- **How to create tea blends.** Unleash your creativity and learn how to blend teas to suit your style.
- **Tea recipes.** Treat your tastebuds with these simple and delicious recipes.
- **20 fun things to do with tea.** Discover the many ways you can enjoy tea beyond simply drinking it.

So, put the kettle on and let's get started!

Disclaimer

Please note the content in this book is for informational purposes only and is not a substitute for medical advice, diagnosis or treatment. Always consult a qualified and licensed medical professional for persistent ailments or other concerns. Always positively identify any plant you intend to consume. If you are pregnant, breastfeeding or on medication, be sure to consult with a professional before trying herbal remedies.

Tea basics

'A cup of tea would restore my normality.'
– DOUGLAS ADAMS

So, what exactly is tea? These days the word is used to describe a broad range of beverages. In this book we refer to three primary categories:

1. **True teas** are those made from the leaves of the *Camellia sinensis*, most commonly known as the tea plant.
2. **Tisanes** are also known as herbal infusions or herbal tea. They are made from herbs, fruit or spices. They are not considered a true tea because they don't contain any part of the *Camellia sinensis* plant. In fact, the word tisane derives from the Greek for 'not tea'.
3. **Flavoured teas** consist of a true tea blended with other ingredients, such as herbs and flowers.

True teas

There are only five types of true tea: white, green, oolong, black, and pu-erh. They are all made using the leaves and buds of the tea plant, a gnarly, evergreen bush native to southeast Asia. It grows wild as a tree but is pruned to shrub size by growers to make it easier to harvest.

The tea plant is cultivated and commercially produced in more than 60 countries all over the world, mainly in Asia and Africa.

Similar to wine, the flavour of tea is influenced by its *terroir*. That's the unique environment where the tea is grown, including the climate, soil, weather conditions and the cultivar of the tea bush.

The taste and style differences between the different true teas come from how they are processed, particularly their oxidation levels. The less a tea is oxidised, the lighter its taste, colour and aroma. Heavily oxidised teas have a more robust flavour and darker colour.

A brief history of tea

There are many legends surrounding the discovery of tea, the most famous being the tale of the Chinese Emperor Shen Nung. One day in 2732 BCE, while touring the far regions of his empire, he and his servants stopped to boil some water over a fire. A breeze blew leaves from a wild tea tree into his pot of boiling water, creating an inviting aroma. The emperor tasted the beverage and declared it delicious.

Whether or not this is tea's true origin, the story became hugely popular and deeply embedded in Chinese culture as the centuries rolled on, with many ceremonies associated with its preparation and consumption. In the 8th century, the Buddhist monk Lu Yi wrote the first known book dedicated to tea, *Ch'a Ching* (*The Classic of Tea*), covering the history, medicinal properties and cultivation of this remarkable drink.

Tea reached Japan in the 9th century after the monk Saicho fell in love with tea while studying in China. He brought tea seeds back to his homeland and it didn't take long for Japan to fall in love with tea too. It was elevated to an art form with the Japanese tea ceremony, which is still practised today.

Tea reached Europe in the 17th century, introduced by early Portuguese traders. The Dutch East India Company was the first to import larger amounts of tea and its popularity spread across western Europe. During that time, tea also made it to Russia via the Silk Road.

The popularity of tea in Britain took off in 1662 when Charles II married a young Portuguese woman, Catherine of Braganza. She was a major tea fan and introduced it to the court, where it quickly became fashionable. Soon Britain was importing tea from China through the East India Company. By the mid-18th century, tea had pushed aside gin and ale to become England's most popular drink.

The 19th century was a turbulent time in tea history, with worsening trade relations between Britain and China sparking the Opium Wars. This was the catalyst for the East India Company deciding to try to grow tea in the then-British colony of India. The tea plant had been discovered growing natively in Assam in the 1820s and, after some teething problems, the first shipment of black Assam tea was sold in 1839. Further tea estates were established in Darjeeling, southern India and Sri Lanka. Today, those regions produce some of the world's finest and most popular teas.

Tea consumption continued to grow around the globe in the 20th century, no doubt helped by the invention of the teabag in the USA in 1908, which made tea quicker and easier to brew. Today, Turkey drinks the most tea in the world per capita, followed by Ireland, Iran, the United Kingdom and Russia.

How true tea is processed

The process of turning leaves into tea varies for each type, but they generally follow these steps:

1. **Harvesting** – the tea leaves and buds are plucked from the *Camellia sinensis* shrub. Some tea plantations use machines, but the majority of tea is still painstakingly harvested by hand, one leaf at a time.
2. **Withering** – the picked tea is spread out on a flat surface to wither. This helps the leaves become flexible, ready for…
3. **Rolling** – the withered leaves are rolled by machine or hand. This breaks the cells in the leaves, which releases enzymes so the tea is set for…
4. **Oxidation** – this all-important stage determines the taste of the finished tea. The leaves are laid out in a humid and cool atmosphere, where they absorb oxygen. The process is carefully controlled down to the minute, to create the necessary oxidation levels for the desired type of tea.
5. **Drying** – this is usually done mechanically, but some teas are steamed or dried in natural sunlight. This process stops the oxidation process, removes any remaining moisture from the tea and locks in the flavour.
6. **Packaging** – the tea is then packaged and begins its journey to teacups all around the world!

Types of tea

Let's get to know the wonderful world of tea. With hundreds of types and preparations to choose from, you'll never be short of a new tea to try!

True teas

Black tea

The most popular type of true tea, black tea accounts for 90 per cent of tea consumed in the Western world. It's beloved for its full body and rich, malty flavour, which is due to it being fully oxidised. The robustness of black tea makes it pair well with milk and/or sugar, and also taste great with food. Tea and scones, anyone?

Black tea contains higher proportions of caffeine than other true teas. It can vary widely in strength and flavour, from a strong and malty Assam or a smoky Lapsang Souchong, to a fine and delicate Darjeeling.

Ideal for: Breakfast time or when catching up with a friend.

Green tea

Mainly produced in China and Japan, green tea is made with a unique process. *Camellia sinensis* leaves are dried soon after they're picked by either steaming or pan-firing the leaves, which destroys the enzymes that cause oxidation. This preserves the tea's green colour and high level of antioxidants, vitamins and minerals.

The different drying methods result in a huge variety of flavours from grassy and sweet, to floral and fresh, to nutty and smoky. Popular varieties include Sencha and Gyokuro from Japan, and Dragon Well and Gunpowder from China.

Ideal for: A mid-morning tea break.

Oolong tea

Oolong is a partially oxidised tea primarily produced in China and Taiwan. A favourite among connoisseurs, oolong is a versatile tea that can be produced with an oxidation rate anywhere from 10 to 90 per cent oxidised. Some oolong teas are shaped by hand into small, tightly rolled balls before being dried.

Oolongs can range in flavour from light and fruity to dark and roasty. Some can be reinfused multiple times, with subtle changes in flavour with each successive cup.

Ideal for: An afternoon pick-me-up.

White tea

White tea is a highly revered and minimally processed tea. It's made using only the youngest leaves and buds of the tea plant, harvested by hand then gently dried.

White tea has a light body and a subtly sweet, delicate flavour. It's also very low in caffeine and retains the highest levels of antioxidants among the true teas.

Ideal for: A tranquil moment, like unwinding before bed.

Pu-erh

Sometimes referred to as 'the whisky of the tea world', pu-erh is an aged and partially fermented tea that comes from the Yunnan province of China. It is made out of tea from wild tea trees. The leaves are pressed together into bricks or cakes and left to mature, often for years. When it's ready, a small amount of pu-erh is crumbled from the cake, for one cup at a time. The resulting taste is deep, full-bodied and earthy, with a rich aroma.

Ideal for: Savouring after a good meal.

Tisanes

Also known as a herbal infusion or herbal tea, a tisane is an infusion of any edible plant. It can be made using a single ingredient or combination of ingredients, including flowers, leaves, roots, fruit, spices, seeds and tree bark. Herbal tisanes don't usually contain any true tea leaves and tend to be caffeine-free. They have a long history and tradition in many cultures all over the world, for both nourishment and for healing countless ailments. Popular tisanes include camomile, peppermint and ginger.

Ideal for: Soothing for a specific ailment or for pure refreshment.

Flavoured teas

Also known as a blend, a flavoured tea consists of a base true tea with complementary flavours added, from spices and herbs to fruits and flowers. The flavours can be added during the tea processing, such as with jasmine teas where tea leaves are dried among jasmine flowers so the leaves can absorb the fragrant oils from the drying flowers. The other method is blending, such as with masala chai where a range of spices are added to dried black tea base. One of the most famous blends is the British classic Earl Grey, where black tea is blended with bergamot.

Ideal for: When you're in the mood to try something different.

Tea talk

Here's a glossary of the most common tea terms you will encounter.

Blend – a mixture of two or more teas from different origins, or tea with other ingredients, like fruit, spices or herbs, to achieve a certain flavour profile.

Body – a description of a tea's weight and substance in the mouth, also described as light, medium or full.

Breakfast tea – a full-bodied tea blend with a malty flavour that goes well with a dash of milk.

Fannings – the small tea leaf particles that remain after processing tea, usually used for teabags.

Flush – the timing of the tea harvest. First flush is the very first picking of a tea plant in early spring, resulting in some of the world's finest teas. The second flush is usually harvested in late spring or early summer, and can be as equally prized as the first flush.

Infusion – a drink made by infusing water with teas or tisanes.

Loose tea – dried tea leaves sold in a container, as opposed to teabags.

Single origin tea – tea leaves grown and harvested from one tea farm.

Steeping – the process of soaking tea leaves in hot water to extract their flavours, ready to drink.

Whole leaf – usually the highest grade of tea; whole leaf tea contains full unbroken leaves that produce a light, less astringent brew.

How to make a great cup of tea

'Water is the mother of tea, a teapot its father, and fire the teacher.'
– CHINESE PROVERB

Grab a cup, insert tea, add hot water… On the surface, making tea is a pretty simple process. However, there are some key steps you can follow that make all the difference between an average cup of tea and a great one!

Take the time to follow them and you'll not only make a better-tasting brew, you'll elevate a tea break into a true ritual to brighten up your day.

These instructions are suitable for loose leaf true teas, blends and flavoured teas, as well as simple single-botanical tisanes such as peppermint or camomile. You'll find ideas for making more complex tisanes in the recipes on pages 76–88.

Step 1 Start with freshly drawn cold water

Water is one of just two ingredients in a cup of tea, so make sure it's fresh! Fill your kettle with fresh water from the tap each time, rather than reboiling stale water. Freshly drawn water has higher oxygen levels, which will give the tea a cleaner taste.

Step 2 Use the right temperature

Water temperature plays a big role in helping teas taste their best. Different teas release their flavours at certain temperatures. If the water is too hot, the tea leaves can burn which creates a bitter taste. If the water is too cool, the tea leaves may not infuse properly and the tea will be too weak.

Check the tea's packaging for the ideal water temperature. As a general guide, black and herbal teas can be brewed with freshly boiled 100°C (212°F) water. Oolong, green and white teas need water around 80°C (176°F). You can invest in a variable temperature kettle or a thermometer to get an exact temperature, or simply switch the kettle off just before it boils or leave the kettle for a few minutes after boiling so the water can cool a little.

Step 3 Choose your favourite vessel

Whether it's a vintage china cup or a giant mug from a work conference, everyone has a favourite or two. There's no scientific basis for this, but having a vessel that feels good to hold in your hands really adds to the enjoyment of the beverage!

Step 4 Warm the cup or teapot

Before you make the tea, fill your chosen vessel with hot water and leave to sit for a couple of minutes. This helps the water stay at the ideal water temperature for both steeping and drinking, so you can enjoy it at its optimal flavour for longer. Discard the water once the cup or teapot feels warm to the touch (you could pour it into another container to cool off, then use it to water a plant!).

Step 5 Get the right tea to water ratio

For loose leaf tea, follow the instructions on the packaging for how much tea to use. A general rule is one teaspoon (around 2 g/0.07 oz) per 250 ml (8.45 fl. oz) cup of water. For tea with larger leaves, such as a tisane or blend, you may need 1½–2 teaspoons, as larger leaves take longer to fully expand and release their flavour than finer leaves. When making tea in a teapot, there's a common saying 'one spoon per person and another for the pot' that always works a treat.

Step 6 Add the tea to your cup or mug

If making tea in a teapot, place the tea directly into the teapot.

If making a single cup, put the tea in an infuser basket or infuser ball then place in the cup.

If making a herbal infusion, wash any fresh herbs thoroughly then simply place them into a teapot or into an infuser basket for a single cup.

Step 7 Pour in the water and cover

Pour the water over the tea then cover the cup or teapot with a lid or even a saucer. This helps the tea maintain the right water temperature during the steeping process. If you're making a herbal or scented blend, the cover also helps those lovely flavours and essential oils stay in the cup and not escape through the steam.

Step 8 Steep

It may sound like overkill, but try setting a timer for the correct steeping time. If you've ever made a cup of tea then wandered off you'll know how bitter a cuppa can get if it stews for too long! Brewing for the correct time ensures a lovely, smooth tea.

While you can check the packaging of the tea for recommendations, steeping time also depends on personal taste. Depending on the tea, you may prefer a more delicate or powerful brew. Generally, delicate teas like white, green or Darjeeling need 2–3 minutes to infuse, while black teas are best with 3–5 minutes. Steeping times for tisanes will depend on taste and the type of ingredients chosen. Soft herbs like mint or lemon balm will only need about five minutes, whereas harder ingredients like bark and seeds can take longer.

Step 9 Strain the tea

Remove the infuser basket if using, or strain using a tea strainer.

Step 10 Enjoy!

Sit back and relax with your tea. A biscuit or two for dunking is optional!

Frequently asked questions

There's a lot of fancy tea gear available. What do I really need?

Mug or cup – from dainty teacups to chunky mugs, anything goes!

Teapot – whether it's made from pottery, glass, stainless steel or fine china, a teapot is a handy option for when friends drop by, or for simply giving a solo cuppa a sense of occasion. Teapots with built-in strainers are a convenient choice.

Tea – you can read more about the merits of loose leaf versus teabags below, but for maximum taste and experience, you can't beat a good quality loose leaf tea. If you're feeling daunted by the sheer variety on offer, start with a flavour you're familiar with, such as a breakfast tea. Once you've gotten the hang of making a great cup of loose leaf, you can venture deeper into the wide world of flavours.

Water – straight from the tap will do perfectly. If you become a serious tea lover you may wish to try filtered water and see if you can taste a difference.

Kettle – a standard electric or stovetop kettle is great. If you like a wide variety of teas consider investing in a variable temperature kettle. You can get the correct temperature at a flick of a switch rather than having to wait for boiled water to cool down.

Infuser – tea infusers are perforated receptacles that hold loose tea leaves and are fully immersed in hot water. They are placed directly into a cup or teapot, allowing the tea leaves to circulate in the water and release their flavour, while keeping the tea leaves contained. When the tea is ready, you simply remove the infuser.

There are many types available, from basket-style infusers that sit in a cup to ball-style infusers that float inside a teapot.

Strainer – strainers are handy if you're making a larger quantity of tea in a teapot. Some teapots have built-in strainers or you can use a separate metal one that rests on the rim of the cup ready to catch the loose tea leaves as you pour.

French press – usually used for making coffee, this is also a handy device for making herbal tisanes. Glass ones are best so you can watch the steeping action. Once it's ready, all you need to do is plunge and pour!

Timer – smartphone or kitchen timers work well, or you can purchase hourglass-style tea timers and watch the sands trickle down the seconds to your perfectly brewed cuppa.

How do I store loose leaf tea?
Like coffee, tea needs to be stored correctly to ensure it stays fresh and flavourful. Tea leaves are easily degraded by light, heat, air and moisture, so store them in a tea caddy with an airtight lid or in a resealable pouch and keep in a cool cupboard away from direct light.

What about teabags?

It comes down to personal choice. There's no denying the convenience of teabags – they're fast, portable, easy to use and don't require any extra equipment. There are also many high-quality bagged teas available on the market today that are comparable to loose leaf. Plastic-free and biodegradable teabags are becoming more common too.

That said, it's hard to beat the quality of loose leaf tea. Teabags also have limited space, so the tea leaves inside are generally much smaller. Thus the tea has less room to move as it brews and it's easier to over steep. The larger leaves of loose leaf tea tend to make a cuppa that's more subtle and balanced.

When you're busting for a quick mug of nice strong black tea, you can't go wrong with a classic teabag. But if you're interested in tasting more of the tea itself, and embracing the slower-pace ritual of the brewing process, give loose leaf a go!

Is it sacrilege to add milk and/or sugar?

Tea is all about personal taste, so there is no tea snobbery here! That said, milk works best with full-flavoured black teas such as Assam or English Breakfast, or a masala chai blend. It's not suitable for delicate teas like white, green or Darjeeling.

Can I re-steep tea leaves?

Yes! Most teas retain their flavour well when steeped again. Experiment with different teas and see if you like the taste the second time around. Green and white teas work particularly well. You may find you need to use less water as there's not as much flavour to be extracted from the leaves. Be sure to re-steep within a couple of hours from the first cup as the leaves start to break down after their first dunking.

Tea for health and wellbeing

'Tea is to the body as music is to the soul.'
– EARLENE GREY

People all over the world have been drinking tea and tisanes for thousands of years, and not just because they taste great. They are revered for their health and wellbeing benefits too.

Tea has been widely researched in recent years, particularly green and black teas. Studies have found evidence of significant health benefits, including boosting the immune system and fighting off inflammation, but the scientific community and health professionals are sometimes divided over the findings. For example, on whether the benefits found are actually caused by the tea itself, or if the tea drinkers simply lead healthier lifestyles.

What we do know for sure is that the ingredients in teas and tisanes contain many nutritious properties and that millions of people find comfort and relief from various ailments by drinking them.

And of course, tea is also a delicious way to stay hydrated!

Let's take a look at some of the most popular ingredients and the goodness they can bring to your cuppa.

True teas

All the true teas derived from the *Camellia sinensis* plant contain powerful antioxidants known as flavonoids. Along with tea, flavonoids can be found in vegetables, fruits, red wine and dark chocolate. Consuming them regularly as part of a balanced diet may potentially help reduce some risk factors for heart disease.

Green tea, often dubbed 'the healthiest beverage on the planet', has particularly high levels of antioxidants. It also contains an amino acid known as L-theanine. This amino acid slows the absorption of caffeine, which means the energy boost from drinking green tea is longer-lasting and more steady than that from a cup of coffee. You'll get increased focus and energy without the caffeine crash. How's that for a productivity boost?

Green tea has even been linked with better-smelling breath. Researchers from the University of British Columbia, Canada, measured the level of smelly compounds in people's mouths after they were given green tea powder. Green tea outperformed mints, chewing gum and parsley-seed oil in the study.

Rooibos

Rooibos tea is considered a tisane, as it's made by infusing the leaves of the South African red bush plant. Rooibos is packed with vitamins, minerals and antioxidant-rich polyphenols. It's also caffeine-free. With an earthy and naturally sweet flavour, rooibos is delicious on its own or with a splash of milk or squeeze of lemon.

Ginger

Warm and zesty, ginger has traditionally been hailed for its health benefits and is one of the most popular ingredients for tisanes. It's well known as an anti-nausea treatment and may help pregnant people suffering from morning sickness. Ginger contains key phytonutrients known as gingerols, and research has shown that when ginger is drunk as a tea it can have an antimicrobial and anti-inflammatory effect. You can make tea with both fresh or dried ginger, with fresh delivering a more intense flavour.

Peppermint

Like ginger, peppermint is a go-to ingredient in tisanes for soothing digestive discomfort. While most research has been conducted on the peppermint oil extracted from the plant, peppermint tea has long been used to help with bloating, nausea, menstrual cramps and, of course, that minty taste is used to freshen the breath. The fresh menthol scent of peppermint may also bring relief to blocked sinuses.

Camomile

Camomile is one of the oldest documented medicinal plants, stretching back to ancient Egypt. Naturally caffeine-free, camomile can be a calming and comforting drink to help wind down at bedtime. It may also help ease premenstrual symptoms thanks to its anti-inflammatory and anti-anxiety properties, according to a review published in the Journal of Pharmacopuncture.

Lemon verbena

Hailing from South America, lemon verbena is a favourite for tisanes with its delicate citrus aroma and refreshing taste. It contains several plant compounds that have antioxidant and anti-inflammatory properties. Lemon verbena is a popular ingredient in sleep teas, and may also help with cramps and digestive discomfort.

Fennel

Fennel has been used as a medicinal plant since ancient Greek and Roman times. Full of antioxidants, it may bring relief to a variety of common digestive issues such as constipation, gas, bloating and abdominal cramps. Fennel has a somewhat sweet, aniseed flavour and pairs well with ginger or peppermint in a tisane.

Thyme

Delicate and earthy in flavour, thyme has antimicrobial properties that may help soothe a cold, sore throat or heartburn, and may even help combat bad breath. Try steeping a few sprigs of thyme in boiling water for 10 minutes for a simple tisane, or with fennel and coriander seeds for a more complex flavour. Add a little honey and lemon if desired.

Tea for self care

'When tea becomes ritual, it takes its place at the heart of our ability to see greatness in small things.'
– MURIEL BARBERY

Forget bubble baths or baking banana bread, tea is one of the best ways to practise self care. Accessible, affordable and pleasurable, the simple act of making a cuppa is a shortcut to connecting with your mind, your body and your fellow humans.

What is self care?

Self care simply means taking care of yourself. It's a daily practice of habits and rituals that nurture your wellbeing, from the physical to the mental and spiritual. It can help us be more resilient, so we can cope better with life's stressful moments. It can also reduce anxiety, boost mental and physical health, and improve relationships with yourself and others. Self care is about filling your cup first, so you can pour more energy back into your life.

Why is tea great for self care?

One of the biggest obstacles for practising self care is time. When life is a juggle of competing demands and responsibilities, it's easy to push self care to the bottom of the to-do list. With tea, you only need a few minutes to create a self-care moment. Unlike going to the gym or a pedicure appointment, tea is easy to fit into your schedule… chances are you're making time for it already!

Whether it's a supermarket teabag or the finest loose leaf, the routine of making and drinking tea is a way to slow down and create a moment of peace and reflection just for you.

5 ways to practise self care with tea

1. Add a spoonful of gratitude

Gratitude is a powerful tool for self care. Our brains are wired to have a negativity bias – it's a hangover from our caveman days when we needed to be on high alert for danger! Nowadays it means that we sometimes fixate on what's not going well and we need to consciously make an effort to notice the good things.

Your morning cuppa is an easy way to kickstart a gratitude practice. As you sip away, think of three things that have gone well or made you happy lately, or three people in your life that you're glad to know. Noticing these pleasant moments can boost serotonin levels, helping your brain feel as warm as the mug of tea in your hands!

2. Practise self-awareness

Self-awareness is a big part of self care – it's how you uncover what kind of self care you really need. It's easy to rush through the day without being conscious of your underlying thoughts and feelings. Next thing you know, it's 11 pm and you're slumped on the couch after four Netflix episodes and not sure why you feel so grumpy.

Self-awareness is an invitation to be present and quiet so you can connect to your inner wisdom. When you get quiet, the things that get lost in the daily grind start to come to the surface. The more you listen, the better you'll understand what your body, heart and mind truly need.

An easy way to practise self-awareness is to make a cup of tea your trigger to do a quick self check-in. As you sip your tea, ask these questions:

- *What am I thinking about right now?* Are you focused on the tea or is something else on your mind?
- *What emotions am I feeling?* Name each one out loud.
- *What's happening in my body?* Any aches or pains asking for attention? Mentally scan from head to toe.
- *What do I need right now?* Be specific. A break, a stretch, a walk, a chat with a friend?
- *What's my next step?* After your tea, see if there's a small doable action you can take right now or simply be mindful of how you're feeling throughout the day. It can help you show yourself a little more kindness and compassion.

3. Take tea for two… or more!

Tea has always been a way for people to commune and connect, from a jolly English afternoon tea to the solemn beauty of a Japanese tea ceremony, or a simple heart-to-heart chat between friends. Tea invites us to slow down for a while, hang out with our fellow humans and enjoy the pleasure of good conversation. Here are a few ideas for sharing a tea moment:

- **Host a tea party.** Dust off your best china and your scone-making skills! Invite your friends around for a proper afternoon tea. You might go traditional English with Earl Grey tea and cucumber sandwiches, or do a potluck version where everyone brings a plate and a favourite loose leaf tea to share.
- **Have a virtual tea break.** Reconnect with far-flung loved ones for a video chat. When everyone brings along a fresh cuppa it somehow makes chatting at a computer screen feel less awkward. You could even decide ahead of time to make the same type of tea and compare tasting notes.
- **Try a wildcard cuppa.** Is there someone in your life who could do with a moment of human connection? It may be an elderly neighbour, the new person at work or a friend going through a tough time. It's a low-stakes way to reach out to someone and potentially make their day.

4. Indulge your curiosi-tea

Cultivating curiosity is a fun way to practise self care and keep your mind active! If this book has sparked an interest in tea, why not sign up for a tea-tasting class, check out a new-to-you tea shop, or challenge yourself to try 52 teas in 52 weeks. You'll deepen your tea knowledge and might make some new tea-loving friends!

5. Create a tea ritual

Rituals are a way to elevate an ordinary task into an intentional moment of pleasure. Take a look at your calendar and consciously set aside a time for a tea ritual or two. Where could you do with a break to refresh and recharge? Try these ideas…

- **Early morning ritual.** Get up a little earlier and enjoy the quiet promise of the new day before the rest of the world wakes up. Light a candle, make a cup of energising green tea and sip away while you do some journalling or meditation.
- **Car ritual.** Whether you're commuting or ferrying kids around, a car can be an oasis on wheels. Make your favourite tea in a travel mug, park in a nice spot and enjoy a delicious moment to yourself. Podcast or banging tunes optional!
- **Work ritual.** It's hard to drag yourself away from your desk on a busy day, but a mindful tea ritual can be just the thing to refresh your energy and concentration levels. Whether it's a strong mug of black tea for a caffeine boost or a refreshing cup of peppermint tea, take a deliberate 10–15 minutes away from your screen to enjoy making and drinking your tea. If you can go outside and drink it in the fresh air, even better!
- **Nature ritual.** Try combining tea with the Japanese practice of *shinrin-yoku* (forest bathing). Make a thermos of tea then take a leisurely walk at your favourite outdoor spot. Find a spot along the way to sit and sip in quiet contemplation.
- **Bedtime ritual.** Take time to wind down, let go of the day and get set for sleep with an evening tea ritual. Look for a tea with relaxing ingredients like camomile, lavender or valerian root. Curl up with your favourite blanket and sip away while listening to an audiobook or guided meditation, or simply enjoy the silence.

Tea rituals around the world

No matter where you travel in the world, tea brings people together. Which of these rituals sounds like your cup of tea?

Argentina

The iconic *mate*, a caffeine-infused drink made from the leaves of the local yerba *mate* plant, is a way of life in Argentina. It is drunk from a gourd, also called *mate*, and sipped through a metal or bamboo straw called a *bombilla*. It's traditionally drunk with a group of friends. One person is the designated server and drinks a gourd or two for quality control, then refills the gourd with water and passes it anti-clockwise. This process is repeated until the *mate* is flat.

Britain

We have the Brits to thank for the tasty ritual that is the afternoon tea. It began in the early 1840s when Anna Russell, the seventh Duchess of Bedford, got the mid-afternoon munchies and started ordering a tray of tea, bread and butter, and cake to her room. Before long she was inviting friends to join in. Her friend Queen Victoria got wind of the idea and before long afternoon tea was a regular ritual for high society. Today, whether at home or in a fine hotel, afternoon tea is beloved around the world.

Japan

Heavily influenced by Zen Buddhism, the Japanese tea ceremony *chanoyu* ('hot water for tea') involves the ritualised preparation, presentation and consumption of matcha, a powdered green tea. Every step and movement of this complex ceremony is meticulously planned and practised. Much more than just a tea party, it's about aesthetics, mindfulness and connecting with guests on a spiritual level. Ceremonies are held in private homes or traditional tea rooms and can last for up to four hours.

Morocco

Touareg tea or Moroccan mint tea is a staple of Moroccan hospitality and friendship. The tea is a combination of Chinese gunpowder green tea and lots of dried or fresh mint, with sugar to taste. It's ceremoniously poured from high above into colourful patterned glasses, which looks spectacular but also aerates the tea, adding froth and texture to the surface.

Russia

Trade along the Silk Road brought tea to Russia in the 17th century. Russian tea, or *zavarka*, is traditionally made in a *samovar*, a tall and often elaborately designed urn used to boil water. A teapot containing the *zavarka*, highly concentrated black tea, sits on the top of it. It can be flavoured with lemon, sugar or honey. Like in Morocco, it's considered polite to offer guests a cup of tea when they enter your home.

Tea and mindfulness

'Drink your tea slowly and reverently, as if it is the axis on which the earth revolves – slowly, evenly, without rushing towards the future.'
– THICH NHAT HANH

Mindfulness is one of the most rewarding forms of self care. It's the practice of paying attention to the present moment and bringing a gentle awareness, without judgement, to your thoughts, feelings, bodily sensations and surroundings. Hundreds of studies point to the benefits of mindfulness for both the mind and body, including reducing stress, boosting the immune system and improving concentration.

Tea and mindfulness have gone hand in hand for centuries. Mindfulness has its roots in Zen Buddhist meditation and Buddhist monks have long used tea to help maintain a gentle alertness while meditating.

The good news is that you don't need to be a monk or meditate for hours to enjoy the benefits of tea and mindfulness. You can turn any cuppa into a mindful moment with just a little extra care and intention. Here's how to do it…

Choose a suitable tea.
Start the ritual by checking in with yourself. How are you feeling? What type of tea suits your mood? Perhaps you need the energy boost of a green tea or a ginger tisane, the comforting hug of chai, or a calming camomile to unwind?

Prepare the tea.
Inhale the gentle aroma of the loose tea as you open the container. Hear the soft rain of the tea leaves as they drop into the cup. Listen to the rumble of the kettle grow louder as the water heats to boiling point.

Observe the steeping process.
Watch how the tea leaves change when the hot water hits them, slowly unfurling as they release their flavour. Notice how the wisps of colour move in the water as the tea steeps.

Sit comfortably with your cuppa in a quiet spot.
Screens are not invited! This is your mindful moment to reconnect with yourself.

Ground your feet on the floor.
Wriggle your toes, too. This helps you get out of your head and feel present in your body.

Feel the heat.
Notice the warmth as your hands wrap around the cup. Imagine it travelling up your arms and gently warming your whole body.

Take a sip.
As you bring the cup to your lips, feel the steam on your face and the aromas hitting your nose. Now sip slowly and savour the taste. Is it floral, sweet or spiced? As you swallow each mouthful, feel the heat travel down your throat and into your chest.

Continue to drink.
Take some slow, deep breaths between sips. Quietly observe your surroundings and notice any thoughts whirling in your head. If you find your mind wandering, gently bring your attention back to your breath and the drink in your hands.

Finish with a flourish.
Continue as above: sitting and sipping, breathing and noticing. As you finish your cuppa, you might like to set an intention for the day, or simply say a silent thanks to yourself for making the time for this mindful moment.

How to make your own tea blends

'But indeed I would rather have nothing but tea.'
– JANE AUSTEN, *MANSFIELD PARK*

Tea blending is a fun and creative way to make a tea that perfectly suits your taste and needs. Like creating a food recipe, the key to creating a good blend is to understand your ingredients and be willing to experiment! Here's all you need to know to make your first blend.

What is tea blending?

Tea blending is the art of combining different types of tea and/or a variety of ingredients like herbs, spices, flowers and fruit to create new flavours and aromas. Even adding just one ingredient to a base tea can completely change its taste and shift its 'mood' from calming to invigorating or vice versa.

Black and green teas are the most common base for blends, but white, oolong and pur-eh are sometimes used. There are also purely herbal blends that start with a base like camomile, peppermint or rooibos that are naturally caffeine-free.

What makes a good blend?

It's all about balance. A good blend doesn't mask the taste of the base tea, but rather the additional ingredients work in harmony to enhance it, just as background vocalists in a band add complementary colour and spice to the music, without overshadowing the lead singer!

Like music, blends are guided by personal taste too. What is a tasty, harmonious blend for you may be a nightmare in a cup for someone else! That's what makes blending so much fun – there's no right or wrong way to do it. It's all about your preferences and enjoying the process.

Sourcing ingredients

This chapter is focused on making blends with dry ingredients. Check out the recipes for some great tisanes made with fresh botanicals on pages 76–88.

When it comes to sourcing ingredients, you could start by playing around with the teas, herbs, spices and dried fruits you already have in your pantry. It's a great way to hone your blending skills and get to know your favourite flavours and aromas, while being kind to your budget.

If you're buying ingredients, check out health food shops, tea shops, grocery shops and specialist online retailers. You don't need to spend a fortune but some cheaper ingredients may lack flavour and potency. If the ingredient smells musty or of nothing at all, don't use it in your blend.

You can also dry your own herbs, flowers or fruit, whether they're from a shop or your garden. Dry them in a dehydrator or simply spread them on a tray and leave in a warm, well-ventilated space until completely dry, then chop them into fine pieces ready to use in a blend.

Always exercise care and caution and read up on each ingredient before use. Never ingest an ingredient that you're not familiar with.

Tea blending tools

You don't need a lot of gear to get blending! Here are the essentials:

- Tea(s) and other ingredients
- Kettle
- Scale or measuring spoon*
- Small mixing bowl
- Infuser basket or ball
- 2–3 cups for taste testing, preferably with a white interior
- Timer
- Notebook and pen
- Airtight container for storing the finished blends

* A small scale is great for accurate blending but don't worry if you don't have one, just use the approximate conversions for teaspoon measurements:

- 2 grams (0.07 oz) = 1 teaspoon
- 1 gram (0.03 oz) = ½ teaspoon
- 0.5 gram (0.01 oz) = ¼ teaspoon

5 steps to make your first blend

1. Decide what kind of tea you want to create.
What's the goal for your tea? Do you want a comforting bedtime brew, a health-boosting herbal infusion or to just play around with new flavours? This intention will help you narrow down the list of potential ingredients. It's best to keep things simple for your first blend: start with a tea that you already enjoy (such as a malty breakfast tea or a refreshing rooibos) and choose just one additional ingredient to put a new spin on it.

2. Get to know the ingredients.
It's important to blend and steep each of the components separately before blending them, so you can understand their individual flavour profiles, their intensity, how the ingredients work together (or not!) and their ideal steeping times. Remember, the goal is for the additional ingredients to complement and elevate the base, not to overpower or replace it.

3. Blend and experiment.
Once you've settled on the ingredients, make your first trial cup. Aim for a total weight of 2–2.5 grams (0.07–0.08 oz/roughly 1 teaspoon) to make a 250 ml (8.79 fl. oz) cup. It's best to start by only blending a single serve so you can make changes to the recipe without wasting ingredients.

Weigh each ingredient and add them to a small bowl until you reach the total weight. Gently stir to blend, then steep to your preferred taste. Pour the tea into a cup – it's best to use one with a white interior so you see what the infusion looks like.

Now experiment with making a couple of variations on the first cup so you can do side-by-side testing. They don't have to be hugely different – even half a gram less of an ingredient can have an impact on the overall taste.

4. Taste and observe.

As you taste your blends, pay attention to the aroma, the flavour, how the tea feels in your mouth and if there is any after taste. Is the blend too strong, weak or just right? Is it flat, smooth, bitter or zesty? Could it do with some sweetener like honey or sugar? Would it pair well with milk? Come back to your goal for the blend and see if you're on track or if more experiments are needed.

It can take a lot of trial and error to get a blend right, so keep a pen and notebook handy. Write down the details of ingredients used, flavour combinations, measurements, steeping times and tasting notes. This means you can compare your experiments over time and replicate your favourites without having to rely on memory.

5. Celebrate!

When you've landed on a winning blend, be sure to write down the recipe right away. You can then do some maths to scale up the ingredients to make a bigger batch. Store your blend in a dark airtight container and keep it in a cool place to keep it fresh. Congratulations, you've made your first blend!

Ingredient ideas for your blend

Choose a base:

Black tea	Robust, full body and versatile
Green tea	Refreshing and a little grassy
Oolong tea	Mellow, slightly sweet, a taste between black and green tea
White tea	Light and delicate
Camomile	Floral sweetness
Ginger	Warming, fiery and sweet
Hibiscus	Tart and zingy with a glorious colour
Peppermint	Uplifting and refreshing
Rooibos	Full body, earthy and naturally caffeine free

Add 1-3 accent flavours:

Apple	Wholesome sweetness
Cardamom	Deep, rich and aromatic
Chilli	Spice up your life!
Cinnamon	Festive sweetness
Clove	Deeply aromatic with slight bitterness

Add 1-3 accent flavours:

Cocoa nibs	Earthy chocolate flavour
Coconut	Tropical creaminess
Cranberry	Tart and invigorating
Echinacea	Strong, floral and energising
Jasmine	Light, fragrant and elegant
Lavender	Heady, soothing and floral
Lemon	Zingy and sharp
Lemon balm	Aromatic and sweet
Orange	Bright and zesty, pairs with spices
Oregano	Peppery and earthy
Rose	Sweet and floral
Rosemary	Woodsy and aromatic
Star anise	Spicy with a hint of sweetness
Strawberry	Sweet and summery
Turmeric	Warm and earthy
Valerian	Calming and earthy
Vanilla	Creamy sweetness

Grow a tea garden

Take your tisanes to the next level by growing your own ingredients! You can't beat the flavour and low food miles of herbs picked fresh from your garden, balcony or kitchen windowsill. Sipping a tea that you've sowed, watered, nurtured, harvested and infused yourself is a lovely way to expand the pleasure of the experience.

The key to growing happy herbs is choosing a sunny spot where they can stay relatively warm throughout the day. You don't need a lot of space – herbs do just as well in pots or containers as they do directly planted into the ground. In fact, containers are the best idea for prolific herbs like mint and lemon balm that tend to take over a garden bed!

Herbs need well-draining soil, so choose a pot with holes in the bottom or place some stones in the bottom of the pot before you add soil.

When your herbs are growing well and you're ready to make a cuppa, just snip what you need and give them a quick wash before infusing. Harvest herbs regularly to encourage new growth.

5 easy-to-grow herbs to start your tea garden

- **Camomile** is fabulous for the bees as well as for us humans. You can steep fresh or dried flower heads. Dry flowers out of direct sunlight to preserve their volatile oils.
- **Lavender** is one of the most popular ingredients in bedtime teas. You can make an infusion using fresh buds straight from the plant or dry them first.
- **Lemon balm** is very easy to grow with a bright, citrusy taste. Infuse it with an equal amount of mint for a tummy-soothing drink.
- **Mint** comes in over 600 varieties, including pineapple, chocolate, apple and Moroccan mint. What could be better than fresh mint tea on demand?
- **Thyme** is high in vitamins A and C. Steep a few sprigs in boiling water for 10 minutes to make a tea that can help soothe a cold or hangover.

Tea and tisane recipes

'Great love affairs start with champagne and end with tisane.'
– HONORÉ DE BALZAC

Shake up your tea routine with one of these fabulous recipes! From calming blends and sniffle soothers to just plain tasty treats, they're all quick and easy to prepare. Each recipe makes one serving unless otherwise indicated.

Please remember that tea and tisanes are not a substitute for medical treatment. Always consult a qualified and licensed medical professional for advice for persistent ailments or other concerns. If you are pregnant, breastfeeding or on medication, always speak to a licensed medical professional before trying any herbal remedies.

Bedtime beauties

Lavender & Camomile Lullaby

This lovely bedtime blend has a calming aroma and is also a good stomach soother, perfect for unwinding before bed.

- 1 teaspoon dried camomile
- ½ teaspoon dried lavender
- ½ teaspoon mint

Place the camomile, lavender and mint in a warmed teapot or infuser mug. Cover with boiling water and steep for 15 minutes. Strain, serve and relax.

Cinnamon Rose Relaxer

This delicately scented and gently spiced tisane makes a comforting drink for bedtime.

- 2 cm (0.78 in) piece of cinnamon stick
- 1 cardamom pod, crushed with the back of knife
- ½ teaspoon dried rose petals
- ¼ teaspoon dried camomile
- Honey
- Milk

Add the dry ingredients to a tea infuser ball or basket then place in a mug. Pour over boiling water, then cover the top of the mug with a plate. Steep for 10 minutes, then remove the infuser. Add honey and milk to your liking, then enjoy.

Calming cuppas

Balmy Blend

Lemon balm and peppermint mingle in this uplifting, sweetly scented tisane, ideal if you're feeling a little frazzled.

- 2 sprigs fresh lemon balm
- 2 sprigs fresh peppermint

Gently tear the leaves of the herbs into a warmed teapot. Pour boiling water over them and leave to steep for 3–5 minutes. Strain into a mug and breathe in the lovely aroma as you drink.

Sweet C&C

The mellow sweetness of camomile meets the cosy hug of cinnamon in this soothing brew.

- 2 cm (0.78 in) piece of cinnamon stick
- 1 teaspoon dried camomile

Add the cinnamon and camomile to a warmed teapot or infuser mug. Cover with freshly boiled water, then steep for 10 minutes before straining and serving.

Cold relievers

Honey & Ginger Classic

Soothe a sore throat and get a vitamin C boost with this simple blend. If you want to skip the caffeine, you can use rooibos instead of black tea.

- 1 teaspoon black tea
- 2 cm (0.78 in) piece of ginger, peeled and finely chopped
- Lemon juice
- Honey

Bring 300 ml (10.14 fl. oz) of water to a boil in a small saucepan. Add the ginger and boil for one minute to infuse the water. Add the black tea, reduce the heat to low and cover the saucepan with a lid. Steep for 1–2 minutes then remove from the heat. Strain into a mug. Add honey and lemon to taste.

Echinacea & Berry Booster

Get a boost of antioxidants and vitamin C with this delicious infusion.

- 1 teaspoon dried echinacea
- 1 teaspoon dried elderberries
- ½ teaspoon dried rose hips
- ½ teaspoon dried ginger
- Honey (optional)

Add the dry ingredients to a warmed teapot or infuser mug. Cover with freshly boiled water and infuse for five minutes. Strain and serve, adding a little honey if you like.

Energy boosters

Ginger Lime Refresher

This warm and zingy infusion is a must for ginger fans. You can double or triple the recipe and refrigerate the leftovers in a sealed container for up to a week, ready to reheat or drink cold whenever you fancy.

- 5 cm (1.96 in) piece of fresh ginger, peeled and finely sliced
- 1 litre (35.19 fl. oz) of water
- Juice of ½ lime
- Honey, to taste

Add the water and ginger to a saucepan. Bring to a boil then simmer for at least 10 minutes (if you like a stronger, more zingy tea, you could double the amount of ginger and simmer for up to 20 minutes to really bring out that gingery heat). Remove from the heat, strain and serve with lime juice and honey.

Parsley Pick-me-up

Packed with antioxidants and high levels of vitamins C, A, E and K, parsley is a powerhouse of nutrition! Here, it's married with the sweetness of dandelion and zippy lemon for a refreshing drink.

- 1 sprig fresh flat-leaf parsley
- ½ teaspoon dried dandelion leaf
- 1 slice of lemon
- 1 cm (0.39 in) piece of ginger, peeled and chopped

Add the ingredients to a warmed teapot or infuser mug. Steep for five minutes, strain and enjoy.

Stomach soothers

If you're having a little digestive discomfort, try these tisanes for some soothing relief.

Pure Peppermint

You can't beat the classic taste of simple mint tea, made with freshly picked mint.

- 2–3 sprigs fresh peppermint

Place sprigs in a large mug and steep them in boiling water for five minutes. You can remove the sprigs before drinking or leave them in, depending on your preference.

Spiced Mint

This soothing mint blend brings a little spice to the party.

- 1 teaspoon dried mint
- ½ teaspoon fennel seeds
- ½ teaspoon coriander seeds

Add the ingredients to a warmed teapot or infuser mug. Steep for 10 minutes, strain and enjoy.

Comfort in a cup

Apple pie

Enjoy the flavours of apple pie in tea form! The naturally sweet flavour of the rooibos pairs well with the tartness of dried apple and the warmth of the cinnamon. It's caffeine-free too, so it's a great drink for after dinner.

- 2 teaspoons rooibos tea
- 1 teaspoon chopped dried apple
- 2 cm (0.78 in) piece of cinnamon stick
- 2 cm (0.78 in) piece of vanilla pod

Place all the ingredients in a warmed teapot. Pour over 250 ml (8.45 fl. oz) boiling water and let steep for five minutes. Strain into a mug and enjoy!

Masala Chai

Is there anything cosier than a cup of delicious, fragrant masala chai? In India, chai wallahs sell and prepare this iconic beverage from street stalls, each with their own unique blend of spices.

Give this homemade version a go – you can adapt the spices to suit your taste. This recipe serves two.

- 3 cardamom pods, crushed with the back of a knife and husks removed
- ½ cinnamon stick
- 2 cloves
- 3 black peppercorns
- ½ teaspoon ground ginger
- 2 teaspoons loose leaf Assam tea
- 250 ml (8.45 fl. oz) milk (dairy or other)
- 1–2 tablespoons sugar

Place the cardamom seeds, cinnamon, cloves and peppercorns in a mortar and pestle and briefly grind to release the oils. Tip into a pan and add the ginger, tea and 400 ml (13.52 fl. oz) of water. Bring to a very gentle simmer over low heat. Let the tea infuse for about five minutes before bringing to a boil. Remove from the heat, stir in the milk and sugar then leave to infuse for 2–3 minutes. Strain into two mugs and serve.

20 fun things to do with tea

Now that you've learnt all about tea, here are 20 fun ways to enjoy it, beyond a cuppa!

Some of these ideas make use of steeped tea too, which gives them a bonus life that's great for the planet too. From sprucing up your home to pampering your skin, give these tips a try…

1. Take a tea bath
Nothing says self care like a hot bath or a cup of tea – why not combine the two? Try adding a few of your favourite teabags to the bathtub as it fills with water, or place a few spoonfuls of a loose leaf blend in a muslin bag and hang it over the tap as the tub fills. Allow it to 'brew' for five minutes then hop in for a relaxing soak. Try a fragranced tea like Earl Grey for an aromatherapy experience, camomile for soothing sensitive skin or antioxidant-rich green tea to help unwind aching muscles.

2. De-puff your eyes
The caffeine and tannins in tea can help soothe tired eyes and reduce puffiness. Simply soak two teabags in warm water for a few minutes, gently squeeze out the excess liquid, then place over your closed eyes. Now relax for 20 minutes.

You can also pop the teabags in the fridge for a couple of hours first for a cooling and reviving effect. For an environmentally friendly option, soak cotton pads in brewed tea rather than using teabags.

3. Soothe a bug bite
Tea can bring welcome relief to bug bites. Steep some black tea in boiling water for 10 minutes, let it cool and then apply the liquid to the bite using a cloth. The astringent tannins in the tea can help relieve inflammation and itching.

4. Clean dirty pans

If you've got dishes with stubborn burn spots or greasy residue, try soaking them in tea. This also works great for saucepans and baking sheets. Fill the sink with hot water, add a few spent teabags, then let the pans soak overnight. The tannic acid in the tea will help break down the grease, so you can wash the dishes as normal in the morning.

5. Perk up your plants

Tea is a great friend to plants! When potting a new plant, add a handful of fresh loose tea to the bottom of the pot over the drainage holes. It will add nutrients to the soil as well as help the plant absorb water, then slowly release it back to the plant. You can also scatter steeped tea leaves into the top layer of a plant's soil for some extra nutrition – green tea is particularly helpful as it's high in nitrogen.

Steeped tea leaves are also a welcome addition to any compost heap. Whole teabags can go in too, but only if they're made entirely from biodegradable materials.

6. Clean the windows

Forget the chemicals, tea is a surprisingly effective window cleaner. The tannins give the tea a natural astringency that helps cut through dust and grease. Simply steep some black tea then let it go cold. Pour it into a spray bottle and spritz over your chosen glass, then buff over the surface with a soft clean cloth.

7. Soothe a sunburn

If you've forgotten to slap on the sunscreen, tea can bring welcome relief to skin that has caught too much sun. Brew some black tea and let it cool, then soak a soft cloth in it. Squeeze out the excess then gently press the cloth to the affected area. The tannins and catechins in the tea can help reduce inflammation.

8. Give the gift of tea

Want to convert a friend into a tea lover? Gift them a 'tea of the month' subscription. Available online from various tea shops, your friend will receive a new tea in the post each month. It's a great way for them to explore the world of tea… and get a monthly reminder of what a nice friend they have!

9. Visit a tea shop

Going to a tea shop is like stepping into an Aladdin's cave of inspiration. It's a feast for the senses and it's fun hanging out with fellow tea fans! You can sample new varieties, get ideas for your own blends, or ask for expert help in choosing a new tea to suit your taste buds.

10. Make a tea cake

A cuppa and a cake can't be beaten, but have you ever tried combining the two? Add one teaspoon of your favourite loose leaf tea per cup of flour to any plain muffin or loaf cake batter. The leaves will soften during the baking process and subtly perfume and flavour the cake. This works particularly well with the delicate flavours of a chai blend or Earl Grey.

11. Freshen up your shoes

Are your sneakers getting a little whiffy? Let tea come to the rescue! Simply place a couple of teabags inside the offending pair and let sit overnight. The tea will help absorb the odours – green tea is particularly effective.

12. Soothe your feet

Green tea can be equally good if your feet are a little 'fragrant' too! Fill a foot-friendly container with hot water and add a teaspoon of green tea leaves (or throw in a teabag). Let steep for 20 minutes or until the water is cool enough for you to add your feet. Now enjoy a relaxing soak for 20 minutes. The catechins in green tea have antimicrobial and antibacterial properties that can help neutralise odours.

13. Spruce up a carpet

The odour-neutralising wonders of tea also work well for a musty rug or carpets. Sprinkle dried leaves over the surface, let sit for 10–15 minutes then vacuum up. You can also recycle steeped tea leaves for this job, just make sure they are completely dried out first to avoid staining.

14. Care for your hair

Rinsing your hair in tea is a beauty remedy that's easy to add to your weekly routine. Try a green tea rinse – its antioxidant and anti-microbial properties can add shine and help prevent product buildup on your scalp. Brew some green tea in half a litre (16.90 fl. oz) of water and steep until it reaches room temperature. After shampooing and conditioning your hair in the shower, slowly pour the cooled tea over the top of your head. You may want to flip your hair upside down to target the back and bottom of your scalp. Let the tea sit in your hair for five minutes, then rinse out with cool water.

15. Try a cold brew tea

Bought a new tea and just not enjoying it? Try drinking it cold. Pour a litre (33.81 fl. oz) of lukewarm water over a tablespoon of tea leaves and let them steep overnight in the fridge. The cold brew process can give the tea a different flavour profile, often less astringent, that's particularly refreshing on a warm day.

16. Host a tea-swap party

This is the tea-lover's answer to a clothing swap and is another great solution if you find yourself with some 'orphan teas' in your stash. Invite all your tea-loving friends over and tell them to bring along some teas, plus any tea paraphernalia like teapots, strainers or cups they no longer want or need. Then get the kettle on, gather around the table and get swapping! It's a fun way to try some new teas while catching up with friends.

17. Pamper your skin

Tea can do wonders for your skin. Add some loose leaf tea to a mild body wash to create great body scrub – the texture of the leaves will help slough off dead skin. For a face mask, add loose leaf green tea to Greek yoghurt or honey, then spread it on your face. The caffeine and antioxidants will help reduce redness and leave your skin feeling brighter.

18. Freshen up the fridge

You probably know that placing a box of bicarb in the back of the fridge can soak up smells, but tea does a great job too. Let some used tea leaves or teabags air dry naturally, then place them in an uncovered container in the fridge. They'll absorb any odours within a few days.

19. Try a stock swap

Transform humble grains like barley, rice or quinoa by cooking them in a lightly brewed tea instead of stock (or try a mixture of both). The tea imparts a subtle flavour to the grains and brings them to life.

20. Colour to dye for

Tea is an easy, inexpensive and eco-friendly way to dye textiles. You can achieve gorgeous earthy, antique tones and because tea is rich in tannins it bonds well with natural fibres like cotton and linen without needing a mordant (a substance used to set dyes on fabrics).

Teabags are the easiest to work with here. Make sure your chosen fabric is clean then place it on the bottom of a shallow container along with 10 used teabags. Cover with boiling water and leave to steep overnight, then remove the fabric and rinse it under a tap until the water runs clear. You can repeat the process if you're after a more intense colour.

Conclusion

Tea is healing, comfort and connection in a cup. When you pour hot water over your tea of choice and let the leaves and liquid mingle, you're joining millions of people around the world in an everyday ritual that's simple and sacred rolled into one. From a mug of milky black tea with breakfast or a herbal infusion to soothe a surly stomach, to an Earl Grey in fine china with a slice of cake, there is a tea to suit every taste, mood and occasion.

Now that you know the power of tea for boosting your wellbeing and delighting your taste buds, have fun exploring and experimenting with all the varieties, preparations and flavours on offer. Whether you seek a moment of peace on a busy day, some relief from an ailment or an excuse for a chat with a friend, remember that it is always a good time for a cuppa!